THE ASPECT OF
Love Life

NATASA TO

Copyright © 2023 Natasa To.

All rights reserved. No part of this book may be reproduced, stored, or transmitted by any means—whether auditory, graphic, mechanical, or electronic—without written permission of both publisher and author, except in the case of brief excerpts used in critical articles and reviews. Unauthorized reproduction of any part of this work is illegal and is punishable by law.

ISBN: 979-8-88640-905-5 (sc)
ISBN: 979-8-88640-906-2 (hc)
ISBN: 979-8-88640-907-9 (e)

Because of the dynamic nature of the Internet, any web addresses or links contained in this book may have changed since publication and may no longer be valid. The views expressed in this work are solely those of the author and do not necessarily reflect the views of the publisher, and the publisher hereby disclaims any responsibility for them.

One Galleria Blvd., Suite 1900, Metairie, LA 70001
1-888-421-2397

Contents

You Are My Man From Afar 1
The Peaceable Buddha 2
The love 3
In Pleasure 4
A Love From Spared Time 5
The Breeze In Fall 6
Blue 7
A Dream 8
Dad and Me 9
Feeling Love 10
Shall I Love Thee To A Winter's Day? 11
To Love You Always 12
The Love Dream 13
Again I Feel Happy Within 14
Desire Love 15
Spring Winter—The Love Life 16
Love You 17
Hot Summer 18
To Love To Be Lover 19
Touch Your Heart 20
Love's Teardrops 21
Meeting Him 23
Dating at Night 24
At Moment 25

Morning Love	26
Blueberries	27
My Love For You Is The Desire Ocean	28
The Trust	29
I Do Love You	30
Behold Me One More Time	31
A Love Song	32
Our Longer Friendship	33
Autumn Pleasure	34
Evergreen Tree	35
Sorrow	36
These Sweet Souvenirs	37
Men	38
Fall Rain	39
Love Life	40
You Are . . .	41
Hold Fast To Me	43
War End	44
Do Not Leave Me	45
Missed Moment	46

Foreword

Throughout life, I store information collected from an imagination and try in some way to make sense of it. When I am not able to fully understand the things that occur in love lives, I often externalize the information. By doing this, I am afforded a different point of view, thus allowing me to think about more clearly about difficult love life and emotions.

Art is the one way in which I choose to express my thoughts in "The Aspect of Love Life Verses" Within arts, modes of expression differ, but poetry is a very powerful tool by which I can express sometime delight, sometimes perfectly clear concepts and feelings with events, the love life or two hearts meet or their making love etc...

Intentions can run the feelings as well.

I may simply want to share something that touched people love life daily activities in some way or I may want to get help to express the emotion within the poems.

The poetry within "The Aspect of Love Life Verses" is from every point of views: every topic or emotion imaginable. Some poems will speak the certain love life readers more than others, but it is always important to keep in mind that each verse is an imagination of a poet, of a mind that need to meet the enjoying and satisfaction of this world poetry, of a heart that feels the effects of every special moments in life, and perhaps of a memory that stirs within emotion of the readers. Nonetheless, recalling my yesterdays give joy, happiness to readers in many form of feelings love.

I want to thank Armando Hartley who proofed reading those verses.

You Are My Man From Afar

You're handsome and sexy
I feel weak when you say my name
I love your outfits that you wear
I love the color of your hair
You're smart and handsome in every way
Your skin is like red roses
The way you hug me drives me insane
I love to date you more each day
I like you as my man oh it would be grand
When I look into your eyes I see such joy
I love trying to make you happy for the rest of your life
You mean a lot to me if you didn't know
You are my special boyfriend
I love visiting your city, churches and the sea
But most of all you are the most beautiful thing to me
You are my boyfriend from afar
A man who I want to date and marry
I cherish things we do together while I'm there
I hope you see how much I care
So please give me a sign that things will work alright
Because someday I would like to call you my man

The Peaceable Buddha

I read of the Peaceable Buddha
Where peace and joy abound
And I hear the wonderful songs of the heaven place
Where compassion governs the ground!
I witness of Buddha to know
The truth Buddha promised to show
Submitting my soul to be made whole
Under the Buddha which loves us so
Such love overwhelms my senses
Living in this world saturated with pretenses
How can such pure truth be reconciled within?
And such true love frees our souls of sin?
This is where our faith rises to fight
Our weary souls began to be restored
As the core in our eye receives the Buddha light
How can this be happening to me?
Such miracles we seldom expect to be
Then this thought reinforces my mind
The Buddha said, "Live in kindness, receive the best life in next life"

The love

This is more than just lust
Fueled by attraction
This is natural love
With natural affection
Your luck is more than you
Your luck or your love
Which one you choose
'The Love'
Fueled by attraction

In Pleasure

Passerbys seem to know
We hand in hand and a smile
And discreetly look each other
We can see in our eyes all that: love and pleasure
I've confessed to him
Though sitting beside you
Maybe even all I've love him
To myself with pleasure

A Love From Spared Time

While sitting with my parent in my living room
I watch the television near the bulk light
Thinking of you my thoughts slowly wander
Wishing if only you could touch me this night

Having discovered your lonely heart
Strangely you touched me from the start
And though we have never met, I do faint
Your invisible pull on me is like heaven's gate

Dreamingly I meditate, have we a past?
From another time, are we now regenerate?
Mysteriously, to you my soul does affect
Inexplicably I know the depth of your touch

Drawn ever more deeply into the love
I see us in a different and distant time
Of a time medieval and unbroken
When taken and died, ever courageous

The Breeze In Fall

The fall breeze bring the missing love
Who's loved the dream of the lonely heart?
When we met far away, waiting always
How long we can hold hands in hands?

The sunshine of autumn missing love
Bluebird and flowers bring our souls to wake
Love fall mix with breeze and color full leaves
World will wake up with peace at the breeze of autumn

The sunshine blow the colorful leaves
Flied my soul thirsty of love
Oh, my lover! How long we met?
Or our lonely souls always had the missing love
Of the fall never stop the breeze and
Our love is always missing

Blue

If blue was the only color in world love . . .
You would love to see "blue skies, stars and moon light . . ."
You would sing:
"The blue skies are everywhere all the beautiful sunshine morning"
And you would drink blue juice for the dinner.
You'd stay in the beach all day long with blue ocean
Cross the bar when the light turned blue
Visit the beautiful mountain at Denver in the blue club
You could even write a poem that starts:
Skies are blue, ocean is blue water . . .
It's a good thing there is blue color like world "peace"

A Dream

The moonlight beyond the blue skies
Stars are calm that night
With our true love
They seem to touch me heavenly dream

Dad and Me

Up in his room, my dad has a very great picture of Ly Bach
That was his when he was young.
In my room, I have my old picture call Connie
That was mine when I was little
Dad never hangs the great picture of Ly Bach any more
And I don't hang my old picture Connie
But Dad doesn't want to throw his old picture of Ly Bach
I don't want to throw away my old picture Connie either
We just want to keep them like the things we loved
If you ask why
We say we don't know why, we just love to keep them

Feeling Love

Feeling love, space full of roses
Who have my love life's nose?
Thoughts in my soul making me smile
I sit here at night wondering and staying a while
The happiness that I'm feeling, won't go away
It doesn't matter, what people say
Tell me to move in, forget or portray
Could you, I ask, if he pays
Sweet souvenirs in my mind, I have low salary
As I write my poems, I bought food with low calories
The joy, pleasure and I delight of his beauty
The feeling love and pleasure as I felt
As heaven 's gate welcome us
To the blue skies beyond the full moon
As wait us in the dream love
As feeling love welcome our love

Shall I Love Thee To A Winter's Day?

Shall I love thee to a winter's day?
Thou art lovelier and more powerful
Storm snows do shake the darling wind of December
Winter's lease hath all too long a wind
Sometime too cold the eye of heaven shines
Often is his eyes complexion dimmed
Every affair from affair sometime declines
By chance, or nature's changing course untrimmed
But the eternal winter shall not fade
Nor lose possession of that affair their own
Nor shall keep thou wand' rest in his dream
Then in eternal times to time that grown
So long as men can feel or eyes can watch
So long love this, and this gives life to thee

To Love You Always

Look inside my eyes,
my face, my body and my mind.
A very special moment,
another make love in time.
Where stars gaze at the moon,
shining brightly from above,
It's here the musics begins
that lovers dance.

At first we will start slowly,
wrapped in each other's hands.
Touching bodies, dancing and hold
for special moment in time.
You kiss me or move a little
closer, love you always.

You hold me, oh so tender,
you lay your lovely face in to my breasts
and listen to my heart and spirits do
embrace, awaken is our passion.

The Love Dream

Like bluebird sang to the moon's gate
I am love the moon.
Desire love to attract to you.
You are like the honey of the bees
and the steadiness of the moon surprises
anyone who has ever seen.
How beautiful flowers and bluebirds
meet and if coaxed will land on my index finger
peaceably but briefly
before the bees or bluebirds land.
The love dreams found within them
If you were my lover,
I would search the flowers for you
and find you in the bulk light of moonlight
for an hour.
I would replace my deep moments
into your desire dreams
slowly and gently to
touch your heart
and would love you with your desire dreams
as you unfolded elegantly
in rhythmic synchronicity
with the setting sun and moonlight In love dreams

Again I Feel Happy Within

Happy in my mind I feel you're closed from me
to let you know to bear my many joy.
I feel as if I am singing in-group of friends
and there must be you see or hear my deepest happiness.

I feel this way more in the afternoon
and the silence day's time seems to give.
The feelings of happiness seem to just appear
they cause different effects to how I live.

There is the feeling that I can let you know
I can't explain the emotions that deeply within me.
I search for a cause for this joy inside
that makes me feel so much love in a tall tower.

A tower that feels like a big house
Never have to give up these deep emotions.
I have found peace only in moments of sleep
that happen causing many wish of Desire ocean

Is this my life I am forced to live
or will I find comfort in my world here.
There are truth answers that I can see
only love and happiness with much future bright cheer

Desire Love

Can your heart touch me with desire?
Love me deeply within from the heart?
Can you wake up and love me every morning
Down to your heart and let me be lover?
Allow my purity to meet to the unknown desire love,
like the bluebird who sings the love song?
Can you open your widely arms to hold me closed
Or will you wish as if your heart starts to beat?
The desire love can hold us within
So our desire love still strongly likes the ocean.

Spring Winter—The Love Life

Love is like the sweet rose bloom in springtime
And it will still bloom until summer
The silky desire is very delicious love
Of two lovers's hearts
With his lips kissed her lips
Hand in hand to
Make the dream come true
And product the wedding's dream
To the true family of their children.

The sweet roses like The Love Life Verses
Its summer's blossoms scent the blue skies
Yet wait till winter comes once again
And who will call the roses to be bloomed?

The white snow in your hand
Fill up the joy in his warm heart
That, when December start to chill
He may still long miss the sweet love of spring.

Love You

Walking the long way in the bright light,
here my friend comes in the house,
I watch him pull and push the front door so heavy, brown, old
New so lovely world, sound and songs are so marvelous.
We hands in hands, then kiss.
I feel his entire body-weight on my body,
his mouth is on my mouth, pulling me toward new life.
The gleaming of my dreams and he loves
with lot of the touch in our souls.
We become friendship in that lovely within the second.
The lovely time is gone with embrace and
continue like the delicious love.
When he is gone for several months.
His touch is still strong in mine.
My love desire is in me longer
from his love for me deep into the rainbow.

I must accept it like the soft love
that his soft hands, his black eyes,
the miracle of him, and of the heaven's gate itself,
making me fall in with him that he never knows
my secret love.

Hot Summer

Risen strawberries
From yesterday's bright sunshine
And the magical moment sun
Bright be together with my lover
Under the evergreen trees
Beneath the blueberries, fresh tomatoes
With the grasshopper flied, their sound
With their ears and eyes listen the music
At heaven's shine of the earth.
I went to school with my lover with lot of love as
The sunset passed by.
He and I can see the butterflies
With the lavender air and
I long remember never forget
Him running with the duck and swimming
With me.
I found myself the secret love with him
forever and always

To Love To Be Lover

I shall be with you, forever true.
As sure as happy of love shall forever
And lovely skies flied as world goes by.

For you shall not tear upon the moon shines
I 'all stay in heaven's eyes with your sunshine.
In tranquil forever love shine

I just wish that sunshine would stand still
With it's shoulders as spread as the sky,
So that I can have love true in your arms,
For I now have a warm heart in your heart?

For stars can be watched as my eyes
Can see like the love that
I have from heaven shine
But even this won't diminish our love shine

Touch Your Heart

Come to me in my love, and then
by day I shall be touch your heart again!
For then the night will more than pleasure
the joy longing of the days and nights.

Come, as thought of you as thousand times,
a messenger from your soul,
and smile on the new world love, and be
As warm heart to others as to me!

Or, as the moments of do making love.
Come now, and let me dream the truth love within;
And part my body, and kiss my mouth,
And say: My dearly love! Why you come to me?

Come to me in my soul, and then
by day I shall be you again!
For then the night will more than love
the happiness longing of the days and nights.

Love's Teardrops

Together we loved each other
we first felt one another,
my heart beat and have you;
I love you a lot.
Your love has found me;
It caresses my soul so gently.
Sweet angel, take our love; Hold it close
for I think of your touch.
Think of you as you do kiss me
And feel you as you feel me,
a depress from me; Teardrops fall
From my eyes when we are apart.
The pain I must bear, because
Of my lonely days are longing for you.
A burning deeply emotion pours through
My artery; It bleeds in my heart.
This gift of you has been
Given upon me right now;
I look forward future to
Wash away my teardrops.
Or else life seems loveless
Next to one with you and me,
I have thought of many dreams of
This and cried many teardrops.

Never let me go, please say
That everything will be all right.
When you leave me, be happy;
Spread your wings out wide.
I am captured by your moments,
Taken well away by you.
Oh love, I wrote this; I sang and cried
Each lonely love.

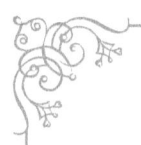

Meeting Him

When I met him
The early morning blues skies windy
Too deeply heaven shine.
He stands at bookstore
While I am at the Airport
Rushing to meet him that is the fifth sense
That I felt him there fingers slowly
Moving to drive awareness
Creeping into consciousness
Of an accident of a melting
His perfume, subtle black color,
of my body to Emergency Room Prince William
hospital that awful day
Bring my life to darkness love
And capture my love to meet
At him longer waiting
Oh love!
I sang and cried for my fate
Of meeting him never come true.

Dating at Night

The deep blue ocean and the long landscape;
And the yellow half-moon so sharp and so bright;
And the stars beneath little waves that leap
In fiery ringlets from their deep sleep,
as I again the rainbow with the hozirontal
And thirsty its speed I's the silver sands.

Then a mile of blue warm sea beach;
Three cornfields to cross till a farm appears;
A tap at the seawater, the quick sharp cratch
And blue skies of bulk light match,
and a voice less loud, through its joys and fears,
than the two lover's hearts beating each to together!

At Moment

At moment, when all the spring bright
that warmed <u>love life's</u> early hour is come,
your loving hands seek for mine
and hold them close at moment at moment!
We <u>kiss</u> at moment to dream
its nest upon the leafless bough
by summer robbed, by winter chilled
by now, dear heart, you fall in love.
Though there are shadows on naked body
And touch my cheek, in truth,
the making love where at moment we pleasure
Deep stir the joy of touching
Kissing at moment
Though fled is very girlish grace
Might win or hold a lover's moment,
despite my sad and faded face,
and warmed heart, you love me now!

I fear not all that moment or fate
May bring a joy heart or
happiness-at moments—at moments . . .

Morning Love

The brightest sunshine morning as I see.
The bluebirds start to sing morning love song.
Flowers bloom everywhere of springtimes.
We walk through beautiful scenes of the blue morning,
the sun is so bright,
a gentle breeze stirs our desires,
Your eyes are so lovely and so warm.
I fall in love with you
for the special morning love in time.

Blueberries

I was a small blueberry once
in summer shade—
deep shadows of sleeping dogs, watchful of
lily's leave and orchid's flower, both sandal-footed and
cold-grass frolicking, issuing to the backyard
world a summer-girl chirrup succeeded by one
toothy boast and one laugh
I was a blueberry sometimes then—
a summer dress made of me, a scarlet flower—
clothed in a blueberry-hued and seed-studded
white-dotted fabric frock,
I twirled and orbited a small place
like the same true flower in warm soil
among chastening blueberry blooms
in the small backyard.
The blueberry and I—
black and dark green, sweetening in summer sun
laughing at the distillation of time,
at the absence of memory then.

My Love For You Is The Desire Ocean

My love for you is the Desire ocean
My heart is the piece of my love passes through
Your eyes and carry your love for thousand years
My love for you is the Desire Ocean
I pick up the piece of your love
Kept into my artery and let it mix
My tasted love blends and nourishes our love.
To let it settle like strong Desire ocean

The Trust

Even such is time, that takes in trust
Our youth, our joys, our all we have,
and I pray and pays us but with heaven of earth and dust;
Who in the dark and silent lover,
when we have the doubts of all our ways,
waked up the story of our days;
But from this heaven of earth, this planet, this dust,
my Buddha shall help me out, I trust

I Do Love You

I do love you because you love me;
I go from loving you to not loving you,
from waiting you to not waiting for you
My heart moves from cold to hot.

I love you only because you are only star in my heart;

I hate you deeply, and hating you because you're with another lover
Bend to you, and the measure of my changing love for you
is that I do not see you whereabouts love you blindly.

Maybe October light will consume like fall's leaves
my heart with its cruel
Stealing my heart to true lover

In this part of the story I am the one who
Love, the only one, and I will live of love because I love you,
because I love you, love, in jealous and sorrow.

Behold Me One More Time

At last he comes, oh never more
In this dear impatience of my sorrow
To leave me loneliness as before,
or behold my lonely soul sorrow again.

A Love Song

Once, at morning, in the Fall Wood
My friend and I long silent stood,
amazed that any rainbow could
Decree to part us, bitterly repining.
My friend, in aimless love and grief,
reached forth and sang aside a love song
that just above us played the love song
and stole our starlight that for us was unthinking.
A star that had remarked her love song
Shone straightway down that loved lane,
and wrought his image, mirror-plain,
within a tear that on her lash hung gleaming.
'Thus Time,' I laugh, 'is but a happy song
some one hath wept 'twixt hopes and fears,
yet in his little lucent sphere
our star of stars, happy alive song, is beaming.'

Our Longer Friendship

A tree has curled, under the sky;
I walk alone, for no friend is near.
Raising my hand I beckon the bright sky,
for he, with my shadow, will make my day.
The moon, alas, is welcome us;
Listless, my shadow creeps about at my men.
With the moon as friend and the shadow as my day
I must make love before the spring is spent.
To the songs I sing the moon;
In the dance I weave my shadow tangles and breaks.
While we were dance, three men shared the fun;
Now we are walking, each goes his way.
May we long share our odd, inanimate feast,
and meet at last on the cloudy mountain of the sky

Autumn Pleasure

Rolling warms soils of a red-orange
spectrum leaves in with colorful
dignity the gentle arrival of a
fall season . . .
Trees rain swirling waves of color—
Quickly approaching their fall's
color leaves in the coming of
the breeze and silence of autumn . . .
The soft whisper of morning's fall
weaves its way across the land,
upon silhouettes of ancient shadows . . .
The grass sparkle with colorful
leaves; A heavenly appears to
the dim skies, as the sunlight
illuminates autumn's delicate frost . . .
Floating atop a deep blue lake . . .
And all the fallen leaves on the
ground to one love's autumn
pleasure

Evergreen Tree

Beneath the soil and fresh air you plant
Wishing and waiting for the sun and rain
A hundred years, with its great roots
Embedded in rich soil,
It held its own among the other tree
And never lost its greenness
Its green and heavy branches
Tell of fresh air and oxygen
Lord, your presence clearly shows
The passing years and
how the evergreen stood against the wind, snow

Sorrow

people muttering with sorrow
of the youngness
my friend now speak
with unthinking why must
my own sorrow unpaged
time is falling apart
my native country now without humanity
out for help why
why must my life
untold
time.
Where am I am now
to stand of sorrow . . . .

These Sweet Souvenirs

I had long remembered those sweet memories
The day we settled to Virginia hangs in my mind like
The new season of fall with colorful leaves
And October's cool Fall.
Over the porch scorched by October sunshine,
We sit and watch the window
Him forty years gone, my sister sat on
The couch with lot of toys, frost of black in
Her hair and morns the cries that echo her sleep
For years it stood by my parent's brown
Front door, and during their last, uncertain year
My mouth dry, heart beating, hands shaking,
I wake up from deep sleep
And reach for green watch tell me
It is 12 pm mid-night and in the dim bulk light I notice
The bed that also hold my parent's radio, lamp,
an indentation on the top closet from a cigarette
He placed there and forgot
In the fogginess of evening and drink
Now, thirty years later, my dad was not longer in the earth
My mom is in the grave.
What we need, alone and in the dark.

Men

-Men
Man is sitting in the backyard
Three men sit on the porch, swinging
On a bench, <u>smoking cigarettes</u>
The wind waits to take a breath;
The night sleeps with the happy days.
Crickets' singsongs wrapped around
Their legs; How do blue skies fly?
The bench gently rocks back and forth,
Big toes push against the floor.
Calling themselves like their best friends and
Sleeping in their beds,
Forgetting their work days, enjoying each other,
A lung full of smoke,
Breathing once again the beautiful world

Fall Rain

Let the fall rain kiss you
Let the fall rain beat upon your head with silver pearl drops
Let the late fall rain sing you a lullaby
The late rain makes still pools on the sidewalk
The late fall rain makes running pools in the gutter
The late fall rain plays a little sleep song on our roof at night and day
The fall is as beautiful as I stay in there for several hours
I love the late fall rain as well as I love souls of America.

Love Life

These days are coming to a slow and successful end
But all I need in love life is that true friends
Who can understand and respect me for who I am
Who can care and love me for who I am
I'm always on the run and living from place to place
I don't have a bedroom; I live out of my suitcase
Another day, another day I live to see the next
I mark the great days on the calendar with a big check
A big check to show that I live on to survive
And hopefully become someone in this lovely world
all before I die.

(Love Life is easy)

You Are . . . .

You were the great person in my life!
I never thought I could be so lucky to have you
you were the first to make me smile
and laugh so hard . . . .
And give me such a beautiful look
you were the only person I truly love
I gave you all my love, my great mind
You were all that mattered to me . . .
I couldn't live without you for even one single moment
as time pass by fast
we started to talk all days and night!
Our thoughts changed
our hobbies changed . . .
There was lot of things common between us . . .
We started to meet more and more
you kiss me while I watch the movie . . .
You started to love me more and more . . .
I didn't know what happened with me
I started crying all alone in the dark because I am happy . . .
I went to a walk in the park . . .
There . . .
What I say . . .
My heart is hot
shredded me into happiness . . . .

I couldn't believe my eyes for a moment!!
I was wishing it was just a dream . . .
But it wasn't . . .
It was reality . . . .
What I saw was . . . .
My love was strong like Pacific Ocean . . . .
He loves me so much . . . .
I couldn't believe it . . . .
I ran home crying . . .
Wishing I will be your wife . . .
Next day . . . .
Next day . . . .
He kisses me . . . .
Love starts again . . .
What could I do . . . . ?
I knew why . . .
So I just kept quiet . . .
He left . . .
The first person I loved going to marry me . . .
The first person I trusted . . .
I will love him . . .
Because I can't love anyone else!!
You are so perfect so strong
You make me love you like teenager

Hold Fast To Me

Hold fast to me
For if dreams are real
Life is a broken-winged bird
That cannot fly.
Hold fast to me
For when dreams go
Life is a barren field
Frozen with ices

War End

Some say the world will end in war,
some say in happiness.
From what I've tasted of sorrow
I hold with those who favor desire.
But if it had to perish twice,
I think I know enough of hate
to say that for destruction human beings
Is also bad
and would suffice to end the wars.

Do Not Leave Me

When we met briefly,
it was not me chiefly
that I was speaking.
I dream of love
sent from above.
Our ages peaking.

As drops of rain
wash away suffering,
you are the rainbow.
I am the star
Each day we learn
that now is our turn.
In each other we grow.

Do not leave me
that which lies under
the external veneer.
Joined by love
by the miracle angel from above.
To each very dear.

Missed Moment

Your missed moment does fit my mind.
We cannot see each other anymore.
I have tried to say 'oh lover',
but you will be the one to try
and keep this pledge as before.

The champagne opened chilled,
ready for our glasses to be filled.
The lights are turned down low
and the music playing is very high.
This last missed moment making me cry.

while he knocks on the door
signalled me to quickly pour
the glasses to half measure
I let in my life's treasure.
Our missed moment fill our very core.

Our bodies hungrily entwine
fuelled by the ample wine.
Passions are riding high
as you finally say, 'Oh my lover.'
I know that you will always be missed moment.

www.ingramcontent.com/pod-product-compliance
Lightning Source LLC
LaVergne TN
LVHW041639070526
838199LV00052B/3446